Plants:

Transplanting, Pruning and the Tools Involved

By

W. J. Bean

TRANSPLANTING

NEED FOR TRANSPLANTING

Transplanting is an important operation in the cultivation of trees and shrubs. It is seldom possible for perennial plants to be grown from seed, or even from very small specimens, on the spot they are to occupy permanently. Most gardens are furnished and replenished with plants raised in nurseries, and such plants, as a rule, are of sufficient size to produce an immediate effect, and may be five, ten, or fifteen years old. For trees or shrubs like these to be moved safely, transplanting will have had to be done two, three, or even more times during the previous life of the plant. Then alterations, re-arrangements, and improvements in gardens may render necessary the transplanting of even large specimens. The operation, therefore, is not only one that has to be continually practised, but the health and welfare of almost every plant in our gardens, parks, and woods is, or has been, dependent in a great measure on its proper performance.

Trees and shrubs vary a good deal in their capability of bearing the root-mutilation that transplanting necessarily involves. Some will scarcely bear it at all, as, for instance, the common Gorse; such plants have, consequently, to be grown in pots, or seed has to be sown on the ground where the plants are required. Others, like most of the deciduous members of the Rose family, bear transplanting without showing any ill effects. Generally, however, transplanting is in itself an evil, although a necessary one. Provided a tree is in its right position and in proper soil it is better left alone. That, however, is merely an academic view of the matter. The operation is an unavoidable one, and what we have to consider is the best way of doing it. Fruit-trees of over-vigorous growth may often have their fruitfulness increased by transplanting, but this, of course, is merely a form of root-pruning—an operation that is treated upon elsewhere.

In transplanting, every care should be taken to preserve as many as possible of the true feeding-roots of the plant. These are not the thick, woody portions, whose functions in the life-history of the plant are to serve as holdfasts or anchors, and to act as conduits through which food-matter is conveyed from the root-system to the leaves; the real working portions are the tips of the finest ramifications, and it is these, or the fibres from which they immediately spring, that it should be the aim to preserve. However carefully the work is done these delicate root-tips are more or less injured, and a plant's capability of bearing transplanting well, or the reverse, largely depends on its power to quickly renew them.

SEASON FOR TRANSPLANTING

The question as to which is the best season for transplanting depends in a great measure on the plant itself. If plants are small enough, or develop the roots compact enough to hold the soil in which they are growing in a " ball " to be removed along with them, there is scarcely any season of the year at which they may not be moved with safety. Rhododendrons and allied plants whose roots form compact balls are cases in point. Of course this does not mean that they can be transported long distances by rail, &c., but that where they are not out of the ground long enough for the roots to dry, such plants may be shifted even in mid-summer. It is not, however, in connection with plants like these that the real problem of transplanting arises. They are simply taken from one place to another, with the whole root-system, and the soil it occupies,

intact. It is when, owing to the size of the plant, or its way of rooting, or perhaps the distance it has to travel, little or no soil can be taken with it, and the roots are not only torn and injured, but also much reduced, that the time as well as the method of transplanting become important.

Deciduous trees and shrubs, as a whole, can be moved during the period when they are destitute of foliage—say from October until March. Even after they have started growing they can be shifted safely, provided they are watered during any dry time that may ensue. On the whole, October and November are the best months. At this period the weather is usually moist and warm, and the plants get thoroughly settled in the ground and the roots calloused over by the following spring. This applies to most deciduous trees and shrubs, either ornamental or fruit-bearing. Still, there are exceptions. Magnolias, for instance, which make long, thick roots, and so are difficult to remove without root-injury, are best transplanted in May, just as evidences of new growth appear. If transplanting is done in late autumn or in winter, the roots do not callous then but decay at the injured parts, whereas in May the wounds callous over comparatively quickly.

The question as to when is the best time to transplant evergreens has for many years been a matter for discussion. Plants like Rhododendrons, that make compact masses of roots, for reasons already stated are not in question. It is the evergreens that have long been standing in one place, or those that do not naturally produce closely-matted fibrous roots, about which the difficulty arises. Some authorities recommend one date, some another, but in our opinion there is no doubt that late spring is the best, early autumn the next best. Evergreens, it must be remembered, are never so stagnant at the root as deciduous plants are. Neither evergreens nor deciduous plants grow in winter (that is, using the word in a general sense), but the former are continually transpiring from the leaves, and there is, in consequence, a constant, if not a large, demand on the roots for moisture. If evergreens are robbed of the working portions of the roots at a time when growth has stopped, the water-supply naturally stops also, and there is no chance of its renewal until growth recommences and new roots are emitted.

The reason becomes evident, therefore, why plants with persistent leaves should only be disturbed at the root either before growth has ceased in autumn or after it has recommenced in spring. At the latter season sufficient indication is afforded by the bursting of the buds, as a rule about the beginning of May. Late autumn and winter are, consequently, unfavourable seasons because of the long time that has to elapse before new roots can be formed. An early spring month like March is also bad, because the greater sun heat and the drying winds of that month render transpiration more rapid. It is, in fact, during March and April that the first symptoms of failure appear in plants that have been moved too late in the autumn. September is a good month; also October, if the weather keeps open and mild; but April and May are probably the best.

The very best time to move Hollies is about the first week in May, but a week or two either way does not matter, especially if the weather is showery. It is a good sign if Hollies drop a good proportion of their leaves soon after transplanting; if they turn brown and hang on the branches, the plants are, in nine cases out of ten, doomed. It is not safe to move evergreen Oaks till well into May. Early June even is a better time than April. Hardy Bamboos, again, ought never to be disturbed and broken at the root until young foliage begins to unfold in May. Late autumn is not a good time to transplant them, but with due care they may be safely transplanted from May to July.

Deciduous plants that must be moved in early autumn, or at any time before the leaves have fallen, have a better chance of recovery if the foliage is wholly or in great part stripped off. If the roots have been much injured, the younger branches are apt to shrivel when the leaves are left on, and a serious check is given to the plant. But if the natural fall of the leaf is anticipated, the balance between the root-system and the transpiring surface of the plant, or, in other words, between supply and demand, is still maintained. The same theory holds good in regard to evergreens, but in this case it is better to prune out a proportion of the branches themselves as well as to strip them partially of their leaves. When the root system has been much injured at least half the leaf-bearing branches are better removed.

HOW TO TRANSPLANT

It is important to bear in mind that the frequent (i.e. biennial or triennial) transplanting of most young trees and shrubs makes safer their final removal into permanent positions. This is more especially the case if they have to travel long distances with little or no soil attached to their roots. It is in the attention paid to this matter that the chief difference between a well- and an indifferently-managed nursery shows itself. Regular transplanting is attended with considerable labour and occasional losses, and naturally adds to the cost of trees and shrubs so treated. Yet such plants are much the cheaper in the end. One of the commonest mistakes made by bodies who have the management of public parks and gardens, and which consist usually of persons having little or no intimate knowledge of horticulture, is in purchasing plants at a low price that have been neglected in this matter. Such plants appear to the uninitiated to be better and more vigorous than the others; and so they are, if they had not to be removed. They cannot, however, bear transplanting anything like so well as the short-jointed, sturdy-looking plants that have had proper nursery treatment. The latter give in the end the greater satisfaction, and the cost is ultimately smaller, for the number of failures is often fifty per cent less. The value of frequent transplanting in the nursery is in its preventing the formation of long, thick roots extending so far from the stem that they have to be cut off when the plant is lifted, and because it also promotes the development of an abundance of the true feeding or fibrous roots close to the stem, which it is easy to save and carry away with the plant. For the same reason the following plan (if time permits) is a good one to adopt when about to transplant trees of large size that have long been undisturbed at the root: A winter or two before the tree has to be moved a trench is dug all round it at a suitable distance (dependent, of course, on its size), and as deep as the roots extend. All the roots are cleanly severed with a knife, and the trench is dug filled again with the same or, if necessary, better soil. A season or two will allow of the formation of a great number of fibrous roots, and the ultimate transplanting of the tree is rendered much safer. In the case of old or particularly valuable specimens it is sometimes advisable to adopt the plan indi-

cated by the accompanying diagram (fig. 222), that is, if their removal is decided upon a sufficient length of time beforehand. To lessen the check, half the roots only are severed one season, the other half the next. A circle is drawn round the tree at the proper distance, and it is divided into four quarters or sections. In two opposite quarters—those represented in the diagram by the shaded portions—the trench is dug to the necessary depth and the roots severed. The year afterwards the two remaining quarters are treated similarly. If there is a probability that the tree possesses one or more "tap" roots, the earth should be undermined when the first quarter is opened and the roots severed.

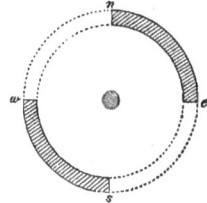

Fig. 222

When a tree or shrub has to be transplanted, it must be decided whether it shall be moved with or without a ball of soil. In the former case the weight of plant and soil may be anything between a few stones and 4 or 5 tons. The difficulty arises not so much from its weight as its unwieldiness, and the importance of preventing it from breaking. Although the plan of carrying soil along with the roots is more costly and troublesome, it is much safer; and it is with a view to enabling planters to adopt it for large specimens that various transplanting machines have been devised. It would be tedious and of little value to attempt to describe the mechanism and working of these implements. Two of them are illustrated here, and their mode of working is in each case easily understood from the drawing. Fig. 223 represents a useful carriage for transplanting trees and shrubs of moderate weight. The ball, after being reduced as much as is desirable, is tilted carefully on one side, the bevelled end of the machine is then pushed under as far as possible and the ball drawn on to the centre by means of the pulley arrangement shown. The wheels should be made broad, and preferably higher than those

ing at the cord another may be tapping the boards close in to the ball. It can be made

Fig. 223.—Transplanting Carriage

shown in the figure. The operation resolves itself into two distinct processes, viz. the preparation of the ball and the lifting and transporting of it to the new quarters. Balls of soil weighing 1 ton or less are best made circular, so that they can be bound up with stout canvas and cords. Between the cords

firmer and safer by tightening the cords by means of a *tourniquet* (figs. 224 and 225). As affording some indication of the weight

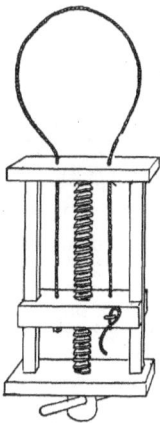

Fig. 224.—Tourniquet

Fig. 225.—Method of using Tourniquet

and the canvas a few thin narrow boards are necessary to prevent the cords cutting into the soil. They may be tightened by making a loop at one end, and whilst one man is pull-

of a ball of earth, it may be mentioned that a cubic yard of soil averages roughly about 1 ton. When the tree is so large that a mass of soil 5, 6, or 7 feet in diameter has to be moved, the ball is best made square, as it will be necessary roughly to enclose it with boards.

Large transplanting machines (see figs. 226 and 227) are only really needed in large gardens, or where extensive alterations necessitate the removal of a large number of trees. Much can be done with a few planks, rollers, and other implements common to the garden by workmen of intelligence and average in-

fibrous portions of the root-system. Some plants can, of course, be removed safely if most, or even all, of these fine roots are cut off, but they are exceptions, and even they would be better with the fibres left on. When large specimens have to be removed, if no apparatus is available to enable them to be transported with a ball of earth, the best way is to dig a trench round the tree at a suitable distance and gradually and care-

Fig. 227

Figs. 226 and 227.—View and Side Elevation of Transplanting Machine for Trees of large size. The mass is raised by means of iron crowbars which fit into sockets in the rollers around which the lifting-ropes are wound.

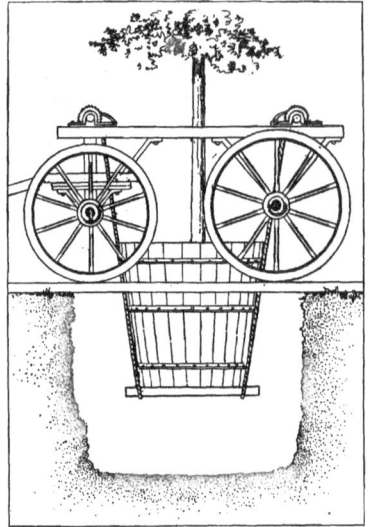

Fig. 226

genuity. We are, indeed, reduced to such simple accessories when large shrubs like Rhododendrons have to be moved. The large spreading tops prevent the employment of any of the machines in common use. The removal of very large trees and shrubs is, however, somewhat outside the ordinary routine of garden work. The vast majority of trees and shrubs are taken out of the ground and carried to their new quarters with no more soil than clings naturally to the roots, and it is to the best way of treating such plants that a few words may now be devoted. We have already referred to the importance of preserving as much as is possible the

fully break away the soil inwards to the trunk. As the roots are bared they should be carefully preserved from injury by tying loosely in bundles. If the process is a long one, the exposed roots ought to be prevented from becoming dry by covering them with a damp mat or something of the kind. All severed or badly bruised roots ought to be cleanly cut with a knife.

Whilst the hole into which the plant has to be placed will naturally be proportionate to its size, it should be remembered that the larger it is the better. A transplanted tree will always thrive better in ground that has been thoroughly broken up. Ground that is to be occupied by new shrubberies or closely-planted groups should always be deeply trenched beforehand. Even in soil that has been so treated the holes should always be large enough to allow of all the roots being laid out their full length and in their natural positions. Any doubling back of the roots is very objectionable. The hole should be no deeper than will allow of the uppermost part of the roots being covered about 2 inches. Too deep planting is especially to be avoided on heavy land. After a plant has been stood in its place, its roots should be first covered with soil fine enough to be worked into all the interstices between the fibres. The plant, if small enough, may also be shaken slightly to further this end. The amount of treading or ramming necessary depends on the nature of the soil. If light and sandy, it needs more ramming than wet heavy soil, which is apt to set hard. Nothing is better for settling the soil about the roots than a good watering. This is best done before the hole is quite filled.

In positions exposed to strong south-west (or other prevailing) winds, a tree should, when planted, be made to lean slightly towards the exposed quarter. Many newly planted trees require some support during the first few months, until the roots have got hold of the new soil. A common method is to drive a stake in near the stem and tie them together. Unless carefully done, this system has its disadvantages. Roots are liable to be injured in driving down the stake, and during winds the stem is apt to chafe against the stake and thus start a wound unless some soft material is placed between them. For large trees a good plan is to use three guy-ropes (thick, soft cord is best), attached to the stem and to three pegs driven into the ground. Where the branches come within a few feet of the ground, three or more of them may be tied to stakes driven in at equal distances round the tree, several feet away from the trunk.

Tools for transplanting, such as picks, mattocks, &c., are dealt with in the chapters on Tools.

PRUNING

The operation of pruning may be performed either to reduce or restrict a tree or shrub to some desired size or shape, to regulate the quantity and quality of the flowers or fruit they bear, or to improve the health and increase the vitality of old or sickly trees. These objects are simple and self-evident; yet it is a fact that, of all the arts in horticulture, pruning is the one most misapplied and misunderstood. It would be correct to say that the hacking and clipping which is so frequent in gardens is not pruning at all. Often done without any regard to the habit of the plants or their time of flowering, its only purpose is to keep them to some arbitrary shape quite regardless of their natural form. Although pruning is a purely artificial process, it is based on one of Nature's laws. Superfluous branches are cast off or starved out of existence by trees and shrubs when wild. In nature every plant, and often every part of the plant, has to fight for a place among its fellows. In the garden this is not so. The cultivator's aim is to provide each plant with the conditions that will develop those qualities which he most desires, and, by removing adverse influences, to enable it to devote its whole energy to his own ends. Of all the processes employed in horticulture to bring about this object, pruning is the one perhaps that most needs the exercise of thought and intelligence and an acquaintance with the nature of the plant on which it is employed. Good pruning may immensely improve the beauty or usefulness of a plant, but it is infinitely better to leave it alone than to prune it badly.

It has been said that pruning should be done with the thumb and finger, meaning thereby that the careful cultivator prevents superfluous and objectionable growths by pinching them out as soon as they appear. A great deal can be done in this way, no doubt, but the amount of attention such a method would entail in a large garden makes it impracticable, an annual overhauling being usually all we can accomplish. The theory of such a statement is, however, sound, and attention to the plants from the first would no doubt result in quicker development and a considerable gain in other respects.

If we consider for a moment we see how untenable is the position of those who hold that no tree or shrub should ever be touched with knife or saw, on the assumption that every plant, if let alone, will attain a truer beauty than human skill can endow it with. In the garden, at any rate, this does not take place. Cripples come in the plant world just as they do in the animal world, and it is as illogical to allow a tree to grow stunted, ill-balanced, or deformed as it would be to allow a child to grow up with crooked legs which straps and splints would straighten. Our gardens, too, are in these days furnished with trees and shrubs from every temperate region of the globe. Thus hundreds of species which in their natural state grow under every variety of conditions which mountain and plain, forest and stream, or climate can afford, are brought together in one place, where the conditions are fairly uniform as regards climate, soil, and rainfall. The effects of this are seen in every garden, trees and shrubs developing irregularities in habit, size, &c., which, unless corrected in time, would render them unsightly. It is in counteracting the influences that produce these defects that the value of pruning ornamental trees greatly consists.

PRUNING OF LARGE TREES

The pruner's aim with regard to those ornamental trees and shrubs which are grown not so much for beauty of flower as for beauty of leaf and habit, should be to help them to attain the greatest beauty of form without deviating from their natural shape and habit. The two great enemies of large trees are storms and parasitic fungi.

The best way to guard against the first of these is to so control the building up of the tree that it can safely withstand their effects. Experience has shown that lofty trees are safest when the main trunk is straight, erect, and undivided. The highest trees known, such as the Conifers of California, the Eucalyptuses of Australia, and the Palms of the tropics, have trunks of this description. A tree whose trunk forks low down, so as to divide the head of branches into two or more parts, is very liable, in an exposed position, to split in the fork owing to the swaying of the separate parts set up by winds. When once this has started, the decadence of the tree has commenced, for moisture enters the opening, and fungi and decay attack the very heart of the tree. It is most important that in the pruning of trees the predominance of the lead should be maintained by shortening back all rivals as long as the tree is under control. That is the first consideration. If the proper lead has been destroyed or broken it should be replaced by tying up the nearest and most suitable lateral to form a new leader, or by shortening back the top of the tree to a whorl of branches and waiting for a new lead to grow. The latter method is best for many Conifers.

But even when a proper lead has been secured, some trees, owing to adverse influences of soil or climate, seem more inclined to keep low and spreading than to develop into tall, stately specimens. It then becomes necessary to shorten back the side branches and probably to remove some of them entirely, so that the vigour of the tree is directed into the lead. This should, if possible, be done whilst the tree is young, for when the foundation of a clean, straight trunk has been laid at that stage, and a well-defined lead obtained, little further attention is necessary. It is surprising how even old trees will respond to the same treatment. We have seen Oaks which, having become stunted and full of twiggy growth, had to all appearance reached their full height, increase their stature by several feet in a few years under the stimulus of judicious pruning.

The proper shape for a young tree of the common type of growth is that of a rather narrow pyramid. As the tree gets larger, the diameter of the tree increases in proportion to the height. Finally, when the main stem shows promise of maintaining its ascendancy until the natural height of the species is reached, the tree may be left to develop itself. Fig. 228 shows a tree which has been allowed to grow without regard to its future shape and stability.

In a state of nature the lower branches of round-headed trees, such as the Oak and Beech, mostly die and fall away as the tree increases in height. Under cultivation it is a good plan to anticipate Nature and to remove them with knife or saw. This prevents the formation of ugly dangerous snags on the trunk. As a rule, for trees in parks and gardens the bare portion of

Fig. 228.—Example of Young Tree that has never been pruned

a trunk should be about one-third of the entire height of the tree. This, however, is a matter that depends on the character of the species and on the form of tree desired; nor need it preclude those charming effects in gardens where the branches of trees are allowed to rest on the ground. It should be borne in mind that whilst pruning enables the cultivator to promote the development of wood where it is most needed, and to prevent the formation of useless and unsightly branches, the building up of all woody parts is directly dependent on the amount of leaf surface. A weak, lanky growth, unable to support itself without staking, may result from too hasty a removal of the lower branches or a too severe thinning of the heads of young trees.

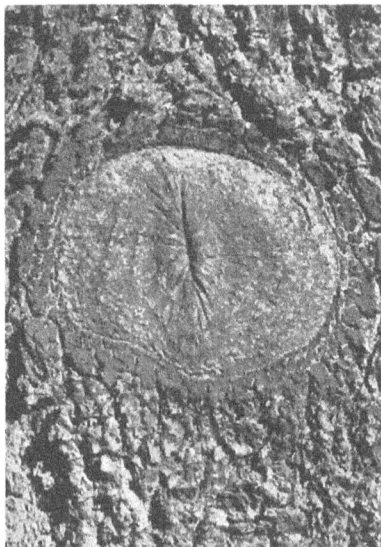

Fig. 229.—Example of Perfect Heal after removal of large branch

When a branch, more especially a large one, has to be removed it should be done in such a way as will ensure the quick healing over of the wound, which in the meantime

because in the event of decay setting in it may do so without injury to the main stem, and because they also prevent the loss of sap. Such arguments are utterly erroneous. The stump will inevitably die and prevent the healing over of the wound. Figs. 230, 231, and 232 show exactly what happens. In cutting off a branch the invariable rule should be that the cut be made in a line with the outside of the stem or branch from which it springs. The lines in fig. 233 show the right and the wrong way. If the direction of the cut is from A to B the stump of wood (BC) is out of the direct flow of sap, and although the wound may in time become healed over, it is much longer in doing so, and the danger of decay setting in is proportionately greater. The line A C is the proper direction the cut should take, irrespective of the size of the wound.

For the same reasons the partial pruning back of lateral branches, which we have recommended as a means of stimulating the growth of the leading shoot, should always be done at a fork, and the cut should be made in a slanting direction, nearly or quite in a line with the branch that is left (see fig. 234). In removing a large branch it is always best to saw it off roughly (cutting the under side first) a foot or more from the trunk before the final cut is made. Otherwise the branch, through its own weight, is apt to split when half-sawn through, and in falling tear a great wound in the trunk, thus greatly impairing the beauty of the tree.

However carefully the amputation of a large branch is performed, it will be some years before the wound is quite healed over,

Fig. 230.—Imperfect Pruning. Condition of the stump at end of fifth year

Fig. 231.—Condition of the stump at end of tenth year

Fig. 232 —Trunk of an Oak ruined by the decay of the Stump of a Branch

must be shielded from the attacks of fungoid and other pests. The thing especially to avoid when amputating large branches—or, indeed, small ones—is the leaving of stumps several inches long. It has been argued that it is wise to leave such stumps for a time,

i.e. covered with a new layer of wood and bark. During that time it is exposed to various dangers. The action of sun heat may crack the surface of the wound and allow moisture to enter; the spores of fungoid parasites may obtain a footing, or injurious insects may deposit their eggs there. Certain trees, like Oak or Elm, are, on account of their hard wood, less liable to injury than others like Lime or Horse Chestnut, but for all trees the best dressing for wounds as a protection against these evils is coal-tar. This is a by-product in the manufacture of gas, and being liquid it can be smeared over the wound with a brush, and all danger from fungi, insects, &c., is avoided. On very large wounds, that take years to heal over, the drying effects of the sun may make it necessary to renew the coating several

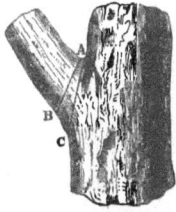

Fig. 233.—Right Method of Pruning. Cut should be made in the direction of A to C, not A to B

Fig. 234.—Removal of a large Limb. Side and front views

times. When applied, the coal-tar should be as liquid as possible. In winter it is often too stiff to use without heating slightly.

Whilst it is useful to apply to the wounds of all trees, whether large or small, the powerful acid it contains renders it unsafe to smear over young bark. It should not, therefore, be applied so abundantly or

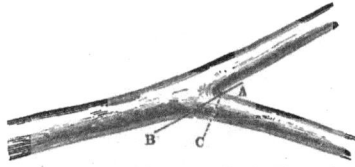

Fig. 235.—Removal of Branch at a Fork. The cut should be from A to B, not A to C

carelessly to wounds that it runs down on to the healthy surface of other branches.

The pruning of dry-wooded trees like Oak, Elm, Ash, Beech, &c., may be safely done at any season of the year that is most convenient, but the removal of large limbs is, on the whole, better done in autumn or early winter. This allows the surface of the wound to harden and the tar to get thoroughly set before the strong flow of sap begins again in spring. This rule should be particularly adhered to in

Fig. 236.—A Healing Wound

the case of the resin-bearing Conifers, which have been known to bleed to death through pruning in spring. Fig. 236 shows a large wound partly healed under proper treatment.

PRUNING OF OLD OR SICKLY TREES

One of the advantages to be derived from pruning, to which allusion was made at the commencement of this chapter, was that of improving the health and renewing the vitality of old trees. A very common object in gardens and parks is an old tree, valued perhaps for its age, its history, or its rarity, with its trunk and branches decayed here and there into cavities or studded with dead snags, and even its healthiest branches straggling, gaunt, and ill-furnished with foliage. Such trees pruning will often invigorate and improve. The first step in their treatment would be to prune off all the snags close to the trunk, in accordance with the methods already described. The next would be to clean out the cavities of all decayed wood and accumulated filth, to give the surface of the wood inside a liberal coating of tar, and then to plug them up with cement, asphalt, or neatly fitting pieces of oak, the ends of which must be left even with the trunk and tarred over. If the tree is not too decrepit, new wood will gradually close over this " stopping " as if it were an ordinary wound (see fig. 236). The living, more or less healthy head of the tree now remains to be dealt with. The chief cause of poor health in old trees is insufficient nourishment. This may arise partly from the decay which has been allowed to set in upon the trunk and branches, but it is more often directly due to impaired root-action. The balance

retained) the parts that remain are better nourished, a healthier leaf-action is induced, and this, reacting on the roots, brings about a permanent improvement in the vigour and health of the tree. See figs. 237, 238, of an

Fig. 237.—Old Oak pruned

Fig. 238.—Old Oak restored

between the leaf-bearing surface and the roots has by some means been destroyed. Pruning can in a great measure restore this. By a careful shortening back of the branches and a general reduction of the head of the tree (it may be by as much as one-half and still allow the natural outline of the tree to be

old Oak that has been treated in this way. It may be mentioned that this result is accelerated by top-dressing the roots with good soil or even short manure. An occasional thorough watering, too, is a great help in seasons of prolonged drought.

PRUNING OF SHRUBS

The pruning of evergreen shrubs merely for the purpose of keeping them to some given size or shape is a simple matter. The true problems of pruning scarcely arise. All that is required, as a rule, is the maintenance of some particular outline, such as in topiary work, hedges, low banks of Laurel, &c., or the restricting of individual shrubs to certain dimensions. The best, and generally the most convenient, time for this kind of pruning is in July and August. With flowering evergreens, like *Berberis stenophylla*, *B. Darwinii*, Rhododendrons, and such like, the case is different. The succeeding crop of blossom has to be considered. With these the best time to prune is as soon as the flowers are over. It is desirable to get as long a season

of growth as possible. For this reason, especially with evergreens that flower rather late, it may sometimes be worth while to sacrifice a year's flowers and prune as soon as growth commences in spring. As a general rule, however, such plants do not need pruning. It is only when they are outgrowing their bounds, or getting out of shape, or perhaps not in good health, that pruning is required. Large Rhododendrons that have been damaged by transplanting, or have become thin and poor in leafage, are often benefited by reducing the growths. They may, indeed, be placed in the same category, and treated on the same principles, as the old trees whose reinvigoration has already been discussed.

Irish Yews, the fastigiate Cephalotaxus, and other erect-growing shrubs or small trees, often consist of a mass of erect, comparatively thin and weakly growths huddled together, and are very apt to blow loose and become unsightly during our winter storms. This necessitates a good deal of labour in tying, which may, however, be largely avoided by inducing each plant to form a central stem and keeping the lateral branches shortened back, adopting, in fact, the same methods that have been described in regard to large-growing trees. Hollies, Pines, Spruces, Firs, and the like should always be kept to a single stem if the object be to obtain fine specimens.

Deciduous shrubs that are grown for their flowers may, for purposes of pruning, be divided into two groups, viz.: (1) those that flower on wood made the previous year (which constitute the great majority); and (2) those that flower on wood produced during the current season, such, for instance, as *Spiræa japonica, Genista tinctoria,* and *Hydrangea paniculata.* It is a general rule with all shrubs that as long a period as possible should intervene between the time of pruning and the next flowering season. Taking first the second group, i.e. those that flower on the current season's growth—as a rule from July till the end of autumn—pruning has to be done in winter, or not later in spring than when the first signs of growth are visible. The later-flowering Spiræas (*S. japonica,* &c.) and *Hydrangea paniculata* may be taken as examples. These remain in flower up to late autumn, and, if undisturbed, the old flower stems will remain on the plant all the winter. The pruning of these shrubs consists in shortening back the growths that flowered the previous autumn; also, if there is a likelihood of the new growths being too crowded, in entirely removing some of the old stems. If the plants are tall enough for their position they may be spurred back to within a few buds of the older wood. On the other hand, small plants need little more than the tips of the growths removed. There are a few other shrubs, like Forsythias, *Chimonanthus fragrans, Prunus triloba,* &c., which, although they flower on the wood of the previous year, do so early in the year before the growing season commences. These also may be pruned on the shortening-back system, because if pruning is done as soon as ever the flowers are over, the whole, or practically the whole, season of leaf-growth is still available for them. Fig. 239 represents a

Forsythia in winter unpruned, with lines indicating what should be cut away in April, after the flowers are over.

Those shrubs which belong to Group 1, such as Philadelphus, Diervilla, Deutzia, and the earlier flowering group of Spiræas, flower after the growing season has well begun. To cut back the shoots of these in winter or spring would be to remove the flowering wood. If, on the other hand, they are spurred back after flowering, the season of growth is curtailed and the succeeding crop of flowers greatly reduced. It is

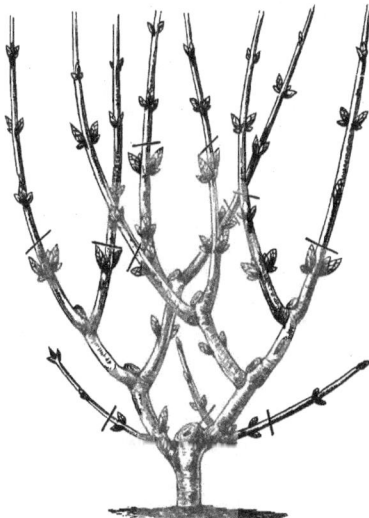

Fig. 239.—Forsythia, showing method of pruning in Spring after Flowers

evident, therefore, that to merely shorten back the shoots would be wrong. Pruning for shrubs of this group must be mainly a matter of thinning out—that is, of removing the wood that has flowered and become comparatively useless, also poor rubbishy growths, and by this means giving the young maiden wood more light and air. The results of this treatment are seen in longer, stouter, better-ripened growths, followed in due season by a more abundant crop of blossom. The flowers are not only more plentiful, but often larger and more finely coloured. The indiscriminate clipping back of shrubs of this class is a common evil in public parks, and in places where such work is delegated to the garden labourer armed with a pair of shears. Such mutilation destroys the health as well as the beauty of many shrubs. No person should be allowed, unguided, to prune any plant in ignorance of its time of flowering and mode of growth.

There is one branch of pruning which, although a matter of routine in the management of greenhouse plants, is generally neglected in the case of hardy shrubs. This is the development of a dwarf stocky habit induced by an occasional pinching out of the growths when the plants are young. It is not, indeed, necessary for the great bulk of hardy shrubs—which, if given sufficient space, naturally develop a rounded bushy habit. Still, there are some shrubs which acquire a gaunt, " leggy " habit if left to themselves. The commonest examples occur in the leguminiferous family. Many of the Brooms, like common *Cytisus scoparius* and its variety *Andreanus, C. alba, C. præcox,*

Spartium junceum, &c., are apt to form a thick, heavy top, with nothing but a few bare stems below. Although, of course, perfectly natural, this habit often renders them unsuited for well-kept borders. It can, however, be overcome by continually " topping " the young plants from the time they are a few inches high till large enough to plant out. Cultivators of shrubs will recall other similar instances. They occur even among garden Rhododendrons—as a rule the most bushy of hardy shrubs. The variety Sappho, perhaps the most beautiful of the blotched varieties, assumes a thin, straggling habit if the growing shoots are not stopped every summer whilst the plants are small.

The methods of pruning for fruit-trees and bushes, Vines, Roses, &c., are dealt with in the chapters devoted specially to them.

ROOT-PRUNING

This form of pruning is employed by cultivators of hardy fruit-trees to counteract a too luxuriant woody growth, which has, as its usual concomitant, a deficient supply of flowers and, in consequence, of fruit. This condition is sometimes brought about by too generous conditions at the root, but more often is due to the hard pruning of the branches. Such hard pruning is a necessity under many of the modes of culture practised in gardens at the present day. Fruit-trees on walls, cordons, espaliers, dwarf Apples and Pears, are all instances where the necessarily restricted limits to which the trees are confined induce a succulent, leafy, often unfertile growth. The remedy in all these cases is to check the disproportionate activity of the roots. This can be accomplished by transplanting, or, where the trees are too large for that, by shortening back the roots during the resting season, preferably about the time the leaves are falling. A trench (circular in the case of standards, semicircular for wall-trees) must be dug at a suitable distance from the stem, and as deep as any roots go. All the roots as they are found should be cleanly pruned off with a knife. When the lateral roots have all been severed, it is necessary then to undermine the mass of soil and cut off any tap-roots that may have entered the sub-soil. This undermining requires some care when the mass of soil is 6 feet or more across. A portion

only should be done at a time, and after the roots have been cut this should be firmly packed with soil before a further portion is proceeded with. In the case of very large trees the operation may be spread over two or three seasons. The effects of root-pruning are visible the following season —the growths are shorter and less succulent, and the fruit-buds more numerous. It generally happens that when once a fruitful condition has been brought about, it continues. The production of fruit is itself the best countercheck to rampant growth.

Whilst root-pruning is mostly adopted in the fruit-garden, it may sometimes be profitably used also in large greenhouses or conservatories where flowering plants are planted out in borders. The same causes that bring about a too robust growth and deficient fruitfulness in kitchen-garden trees may bring about a shy-flowering condition in some greenhouse plants. *Clethra arborea,* for instance, planted out in a rich conservatory border, will often fail to flower anything like so well as when restricted in pots or tubs. The remedy in this case also is a judicious root-pruning.

After what has been said, it need scarcely be pointed out that root-pruning cannot be employed to cure the barrenness of trees, which is due to lack of vigour or starvation at the root.

TOOLS, INSTRUMENTS, ETC., USED IN GARDENS

Many of the tools used in gardens are so familiar to gardeners, that a mere enumeration of them might be considered sufficient here, yet the difference between a good and a bad one, both being employed for the same purpose, is of great importance. The spade is one of the most commonly used implements, and it is not perhaps too much to say that with one of the modern improved kinds a man could do, with the same exertion, 10 per cent more work than he could with the heavy easily-clogged kinds formerly in use. But besides the advantage from more work being performed, it is always the case that, with a well-adapted tool, the work can be much better done.

The care of tools, &c., is a matter of considerable importance, although it is too often neglected. Economy, not only in outlay, but also in labour, is secured by attention to the proper cleaning and storing of all tools when not in use. In large establishments, where numerous implements of various kinds are required, a tool-shed is usually provided, with arrangements for their convenient and safe storing. Brackets and hooks against walls for sieves, ropes, scythes, rakes, spades, &c., shelves, drawers, or cupboards for small tools, and boxes for labels, twine, pegs, &c., should be provided in an orderly tool-shed, and the men should be taught to return every article to its proper place when not in use. Wet days may be turned to good account by oiling, sharpening, and repairing any tools that require it. Even in small gardens a suitable place for the storage of tools ought to be found, instead of, as is too often the case, throwing them into any corner or out-of-the-way place, where they either get spoilt with rust or damp or are mysteriously missing when next required. Men work better when in good health than when in bad, and in like manner with good clean tools more and better work is accomplished than is possible when they are either rusty or blunt or rickety.

I. TOOLS

The Spade.—Of all garden implements the spade is universally admitted to be the most generally useful. With it alone the roughest soil may be gradually brought to a fine tilth and a state of fertility. Although long-handled straight spades are used in some countries, there is no better and more efficient spade in existence than the neat short-handled variety with a D-top such as is generally used in English gardens (fig. 240).

Shovels.—These being broader and lighter than the spade, and having the edges turned up, are better adapted for moving loose soil, gravel, or sand (see fig. 241).

Picks.—There are several varieties of these, some having pointed, others cutting ends. As they are used for penetrating and loosening hard soils or gravel, or for cutting roots among sandy or stony particles, these implements require to have their ends well steeled and tempered.

The *Common Pick* has both ends pointed, and is curved, the curve nearly corresponding with the segment of a circle, of which the radius is somewhat greater than that of the curve described by the pick in making a stroke.

The *Pickaxe* is pointed at one end like the common pick; but the other end is wedge-shaped, and sharpened for use in the cutting of roots of trees, &c. The cutting edge is in the direction of the handle.

The *Mattock* (fig. 242) has one end pointed and the other flattened, the edge being transverse, or at right angles to the direction of the handle. A small form of it, known as the hand-pick, is a serviceable tool when large trees are being transplanted, as it can be used

Fig. 242

Fig. 243

Fig. 244

Fig. 245

Fig. 247

Fig. 240

Fig. 241

Fig. 253

Fig. 246

Fig. 252

Fig. 257

Fig. 251

Fig. 254

Fig. 248

Fig. 255

Fig. 249

Fig. 250

Fig. 260

Fig. 256

Fig. 261

Fig. 258

Fig. 259

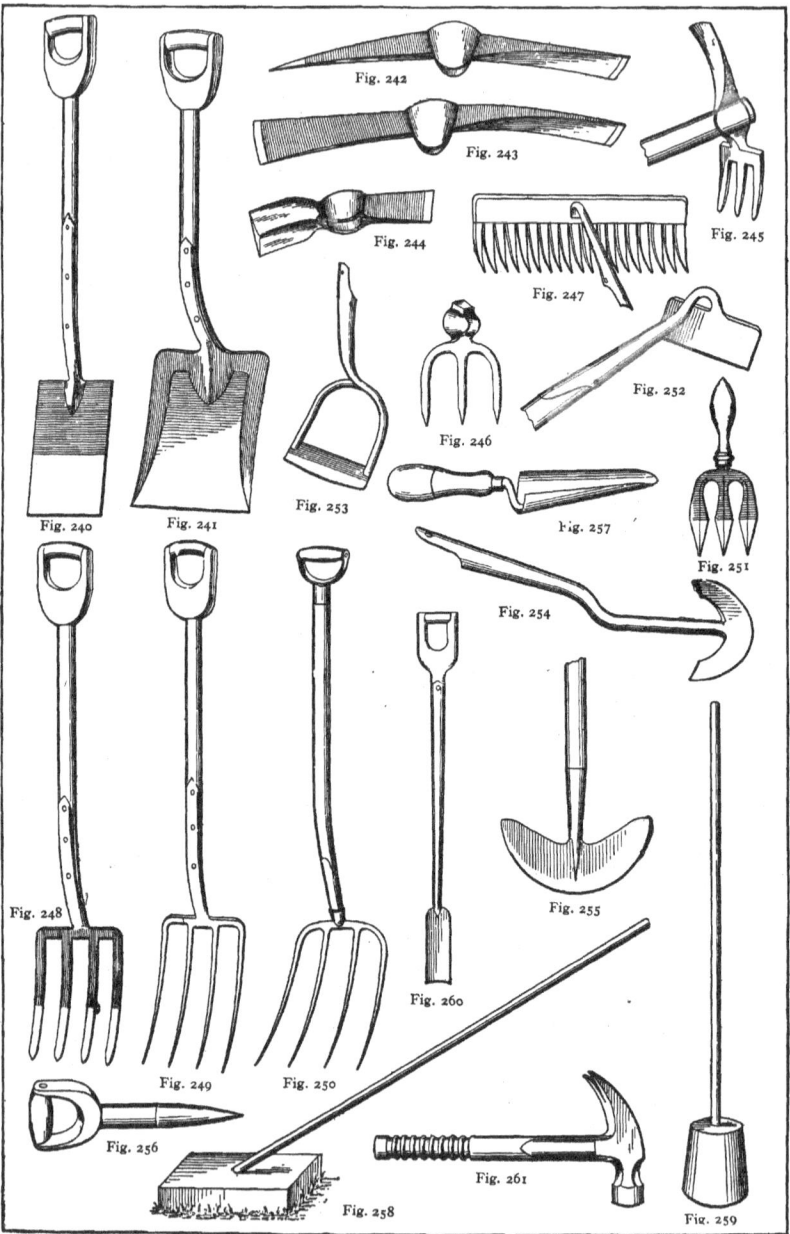

Gardening Tools

for undermining, &c. The length of the head is 10 inches, and of the handle 12 inches.

Grubbing Axe (fig. 243).—This is brought to a thin wedge shape at both ends. It is well adapted for grubbing up trees. A short-handled modification of this is shown in fig. 244.

The *Pickfork* (fig. 245), or Canterbury hoe, is useful for loosening soil. By means of the fork end the surface may be broken up, and when this is too hard, or when clods have to be broken, the mattock end may be employed; it is also useful for loosening the subsoil to the proper depth, where it would otherwise form hard banks over which the water could not pass, and would consequently lodge injuriously in the softer parts.

The *Drag* (fig. 246) is a small three-pronged implement, used instead of a hoe for loosening the soil among vegetable crops in the market gardens near London.

Rakes.—Iron-headed rakes of different sizes are required, the length of the heads varying from 14 to 4 inches. The best are now made with the end teeth formed out of the head and turned down, the other teeth being riveted in and very slightly curved. The socket should be long and strong and three-holed. Wooden rakes, with short close teeth, may be made to take off short grass from lawns so cleanly as sometimes to render sweeping unnecessary.

The *Daisy-rake* (fig. 247) has broad teeth, sharp on both edges; it is employed for removing the flowers of daisies and other plants from lawns.

Forks are perhaps employed for more purposes in gardens than any other tool. They may be used in place of the spade for digging. The trenching fork (fig. 248) is four-pronged flat, or four-pronged square, and extra strong. Fig. 249 is a useful digging fork. The potato fork is four- or five-pronged flat, of lighter make than the digging fork. The manure fork is generally four-pronged round, very light and elastic, with either a short handle similar to the digging fork or a long straight handle (fig. 250), the latter being very useful for long manure. The hand-fork (fig. 251) is a useful tool in many ways.

Hoes.—These are used for drawing furrows or drills, stirring the soil, earthing up, &c.

Draw-hoes have the blade attached to the socket by a solid neck, more or less curved, as in fig. 252. The blade should be made of steel, welded on an iron neck. The length

of the plate for the largest need not exceed 9 inches; hoes for Onions, &c., are required as small as 2 inches. A very useful crane-necked hoe is in use in the midland counties, with movable steel plates 5 to 7 inches long.

The Dutch or thrust hoes (fig. 253) are useful for cutting down weeds, and for very shallow work on an even surface; but they are not so good as the draw-hoe when the ground is stiff and lumpy. The Dutch hoe can be used to a considerable extent without going out of the alleys, so that the ground is not trodden as it is in using the draw-hoe. For light work, and in flower-gardens, these hoes are most useful.

The *Turfing-Iron* (fig. 254) has a crescent-shaped blade and a bent handle, adapted for cutting turf. Before using this tool, however, the turf must be cut into strips by a *Verge-cutter* (fig. 255). Wheel verge-cutters are also used for this purpose.

The " Planet Jr." (fig. 262) is an American invention which can be readily adapted for performing many gardening operations; viz. as a drill grubber; as an expanding drill harrow; as a scarifier for hoeing, grubbing, and ridging-up Turnip, Potato, Bean, and Cabbage; for hoeing between Strawberry rows, and for flat cultivation generally.

Dibbers.—These are generally made of the upper part of old spade handles and are sometimes shod (see fig. 256). Dibbling is open to some objections. The roots are crowded together in a narrow hole. When the soil is heavy, or not in good working order, the trowel is much to be preferred, especially for larger plants. The Potato-dibber has a cross handle at top, which can be grasped with both hands, and a projecting piece of iron or wood serving as a tread and to control the depth of the hole.

Garden Trowel.—The common garden trowel, fig. 257, is now made of steel, united to a curved iron neck. It is used for many purposes, but chiefly for taking up plants and replanting them, with balls of earth adhering.

The *Turf-beetle* is a solid piece of wood, used for levelling and consolidating newly laid turf. It may be formed from a thick knotted end of elm, outside slab, varying in thickness from 1½ inch near outside edges to 3 or even 4 inches in centre, and having a handle inserted in the upper side (fig. 258). The handle should be fixed at a sufficiently acute angle with the sole of the beetle being easily brought down flat.

The *Rammer* (fig. 259) is useful for firming

the earth about posts, tree-guards, &c., and for consolidating turf and gravel. It is generally made of wood, in the form of a half-cone, attached to an upright stem.

Rollers.—A heavy cast-iron roller is required for broad walks, gravel areas, and for lawns. In flower-gardens, or where the walks are narrow, or their turnings intricate, a narrow roller must be employed. Iron rollers with the cylinder in two parts to

curved piece of iron on the back serves as a fulcrum; in some forms of the implement a projecting knob answers the same purpose.

Crowbar.—Useful for making holes for stakes; is occasionally employed as a lever for loosening the soil below trees that are to be removed. A pair of good steel crowbars are useful tools for gardens of any size.

Hammer.—An important use of a hammer

Fig. 262.—" Planet Jr." Single-wheel Hoe

facilitate turning without disfiguring the walk are best. Stone rollers are used for pressing down seed beds.

Suckering Iron (fig. 260).—This is useful for removing suckers from Roses, Gooseberries, Currants, or other shrubs. Its length is about 3 feet 6 inches. The edge is usually straight, and is apt to slip past the sucker; but the figure represents an improvement, the edge being concave.

The *Dock-weeder* is employed for taking up such deep tap-rooted weeds as Docks; it consists of an iron blade with two prongs, fixed in a handle like that of a spade; a

in gardening is for nailing wall-trees. For this purpose the head should be rounded to serve as a fulcrum in drawing nails, and in this operation the claws should hold the nails without slipping. The head also should not be too long, otherwise, in drawing nails, it is apt to bruise adjoining branches, where these happen to be close together. A useful form is shown in fig. 261.

Pincers and *Pliers* are requisite for drawing nails, bending and cutting wire, and other purposes. They are too often missing from the garden tool-chest. A screw-driver and file are equally necessary.

II. CUTTING INSTRUMENTS

The *Pruning Knife* (fig. 263) is the best instrument that can be employed for pruning trees and shrubs, and for a variety of other purposes. There are various forms of it; the blade in some is made with a joint, so as to fold in; and in others it is fixed immovably in the handle. Knives with folding blades possess many advantages. The

Fig. 263.—Pruning   Figs. 264, 265.—Budding
Knife   Knives

handle should be made of buck's-horn, the rough surface of which prevents the hand from slipping. With regard to the shape of the blade, some prefer blades with straight edges; others those the edges of which are more or less curved. For removing small shoots a straight-edged blade is preferred; but where branches are to be cut off, a curved blade can be used with greater effect.

The *Budding Knife* has a thin straight blade fixed in a flat ivory handle. Figs. 264 and 265 represent good forms of budding knives.

Hedge Shears.—A good form of these is

represented in fig. 266. They are strong both in blade and shaft, the former being straight-edged, except a small portion near the pivot, which is concave and convex, so that strong branches are easily grasped and cut.

Another form of shears, known as Lopping Shears, is short and parrot-bill shaped in blade and long in shaft. The upper portion of it is shown in fig. 267. These are employed for grasping and cutting stronger branches than can be done with the ordinary hedge shears. They should have strong wooden handles about 3 feet in length, and broadly ferruled where the prongs are inserted to prevent splitting.

Grass-edging Shears.—These are sometimes furnished with a small wheel to run along close by the edge of the grass; but the form represented in fig. 268 is best adapted for general use. They were formerly made with the handles at right angle to the blades, but they are now made with an angle of 110°. The axis or pin on which the blades turn should have a smoothly rounded head next the edging; that is, on the left-hand side. The other end of the axis should have a screw and nut with a washer; or there may be two thin nuts worked hard against each other, to prevent their being turned by the movement of the blades. It is necessary that the end of the screw should be on the right-hand side, otherwise it would catch against the edging.

Pruning Shears.—There are various sizes of these, according to the greater or less thickness of the shoots or small branches to be cut off. The pruning shears shown in figs. 269 and 270 are employed for the removal of the shoots of fruit-trees; and the centres being movable, they produce a draw cut like a knife, instead of a crushing cut like that of the common shears.

The shears represented in fig. 271 are useful for pruning Gooseberries, Currants, Roses, and other plants.

The *Standard Tree-pruner* (fig. 281) is for the purpose of pruning branches situated at a considerable height. There are several forms of it, but they all consist of two blades, one of which is fixed to a handle, and the other to a lever, to which a strained wire is attached. Another form is the Hook Tree-pruner, represented at fig. 272. This will cut through branches an inch or more in diameter with ease. The Aerial

Fig. 268

Fig. 267

Fig. 266

Fig. 269

Fig. 270

Fig. 271

Fig. 275

Fig. 278

Fig. 276

Fig. 277

Fig. 274

Fig. 273

Fig. 279

Fig. 272

Fig. 280

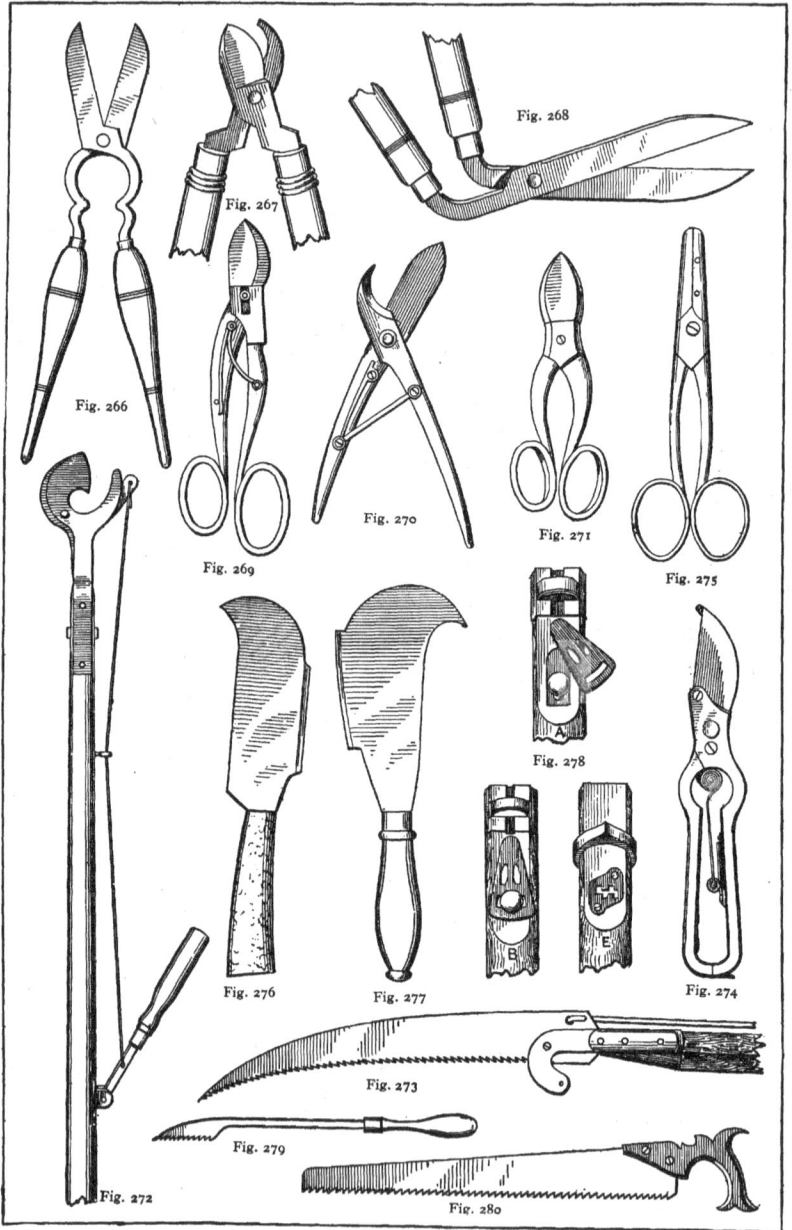

Cutting Instruments

Pruning Saw (fig. 273), to fit the Standard Tree-pruner, is useful for the removal of boughs too large for the " pruner " alone.

The *Sécateur* (fig. 274) is a French invention to replace the pruning knife, for pruning roses, fruit-trees, &c.

The *Flower Gatherer* (fig. 275) is a useful form of scissors, with blades so constructed as to hold the flower after it has been severed.

Grape Scissors, used for thinning bunches of Grapes, have small tapering blunt points, to prevent pricking the berries.

The Axe.—One of a convenient size is useful for many garden purposes, and a large one, with a handle long enough to be used with both hands, is required for felling trees.

The Hedge or Pruning Bill.—This instrument is employed for dressing the sides of hedges. It is a slightly curved blade, attached to a handle about 4 feet long.

The *Bill-hook* (figs. 276 and 277) is used instead of the axe for many purposes. It varies in form in different districts or counties, the blades being more curved or longer in one district than in another.

Scythe.—The usual form of scythe-blade answers for lawns, provided the neck is set with the handle to take in a wider sweep, and it should also be turned up so that the under side of the blade may be nearly flat with the surface of the ground. The scythe-snaths (fig. 278) are an improved method of attaching the blade to the shaft. Much depends on the placing of the two projecting handles for the grasp; their distance from the heel, and from each other, should be so regulated that the blade, when lifted up clear off the ground, will balance parallel to the surface.

The *Asparagus Knife* (fig. 279) has a serrated steel blade, with long iron shank fixed in a wooden handle. It is pushed down and the shoot is cut, or rather sawed off, near its base.

Saws.—A cross-cut saw is required for cutting down trees; for large limbs the saws used by carpenters will answer, only the teeth may require to be wider set if the wood is soft and full of sap. Pruning saws (fig. 280) are adapted for cutting close to the fork of branches, or where a broader blade could not be introduced.

Before saws used in pruning are laid aside,

Fig. 281.—Standard Tree-pruner in use

they should, in the first place, be perfectly cleaned from all juice, or other adhesive substance, that may collect upon their surface. They should then be well dried and oiled. They will also work more easily, and cut more expeditiously and with less danger of breaking, if cleaned and oiled occasionally when in use.

III. INSTRUMENTS USED IN LAYING OUT GROUND LINES

Garden Line and Reel.—A garden line should be of good material, wound on a reel, which not only permits the line to dry more speedily than when closely rolled up, but also facilitates its being readily extended and re-coiled. When stretched and supported between two points, with the intention of indicating a straight line between them, the line should combine strength with lightness, as, for instance, small whip-cord. A stout iron pin, 2 feet long, with a loop after the pattern of a skewer, is a useful fastener for a garden line.

The *Chain* is indispensable where land,

walks, or roads have to be measured, and it is always desirable that there should be one in a garden of considerable extent. Gunter's chain consists of 100 links, each of which is 7·92 inches in length, consequently the whole length of the chain is 66 feet = 22 yards, or 4 poles.

Accompanying the chain are ten small arrows, about 15 inches in length, the use of which is to mark the termination of each chain's length.

Measuring-rods.—Two thin rods, such as are used by surveyors, are useful for accurate measurements; but for common use in the open ground a 10-foot rod of clean, well-seasoned deal, about 1¼ inch square, with each foot clearly marked and numbered, may be substituted. A copper fastening should be put round each end, to prevent splitting and wearing.

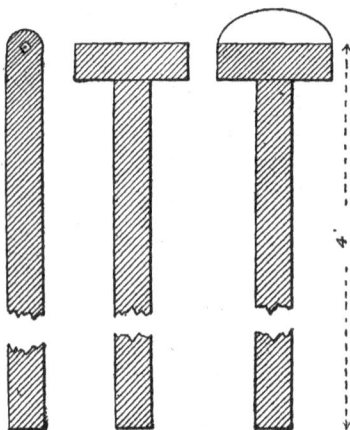

Fig. 282.—Borning-rods

Stakes.—Often required for marking out lines for walks, boundaries, and divisions, or when plantations, edgings, and lines have to be made out afresh. They should be 6 feet in length, 1 inch square, quite straight, and the lower end regularly pointed. When not in use, they should be kept in a dry place, strapped together in bundles.

Borning-rods.—These usually consist of three straight rods of equal length, each with a cross-piece at right angles across the top. They are used for determining points that shall be either in a horizontal or uniformly inclined plane.

A set shown in fig. 282 will be found handy and accurate. The sighting hole is

in the plain upright rod, where a triangular or diamond-shaped piece of zinc is neatly let in; the end T-rod has the cross-piece shaped in a rounded form and painted white.

Ground Compasses.—These are useful in

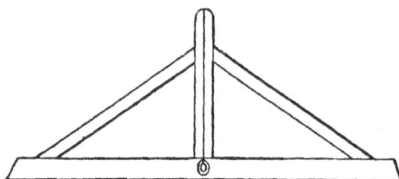

Fig. 283.—Level

making geometrical flower-gardens or striking beds on lawns. They are constructed on the same principle as the common compasses, with the segment gauge used by mechanics.

The *Plummet* may be very usefully em-

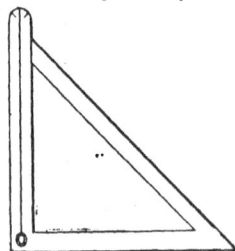

Fig. 284.—Level

ployed in placing objects correctly upright, such as posts, stakes, and trees.

Levels.—Wherever walks, roads, or drains are to be made, or indeed whenever grounds are to be laid out, a level is indispensable. Though the surface of the ground may, to

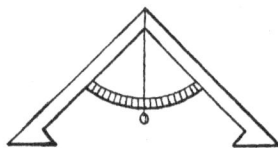

Fig. 285.—Artillery Foot-level

all appearance, be quite level, yet it will often be found, when the level is used, to slope considerably.

There are many different kinds of levels. The common level (fig. 283), used by bricklayers and carpenters, is well known. The level seen in fig. 284 is used not only for forming a horizontal surface, but also for ascertaining whether an object is truly perpendicular or not. The artillery foot-level (fig. 285) has a line and plummet, and a scale of 90° between the two legs.

Where long horizontal, or uniformly sloping lines are to be formed, the spirit-level is by far the best and most expeditious.

It is now frequently bedded in a straight-edge board, 5 or 6 feet in length, 4 inches wide, and 1¼ inch thick. For making walks, the one edging level is very serviceable.

For taking extensive and important levels, an experienced surveyor should be employed, and he provides the necessary instruments.

IV. MACHINES AND OTHER ACCESSORIES

Lawn-mowers.—Since the invention of the lawn-mower, lawns are kept in better condition and at much less cost than when the scythe alone was used. They range from the toy-like article cutting a few inches to that of the horse or motor machine cutting 30 inches. The majority of those used in this country are gear- or wheel-driven. One of the best of these is the Caledonia (fig. 286), a roller machine, which is extensively used by gardeners. Among high-class mowers of the side-wheel type, Shanks's "Talisman" is well known; and another popular machine

The Lawn-mower Carriage (fig. 290) is for conveying lawn-mowers from place to place, so as to avoid running them over gravel or rough ground, which is apt to damage the knives and gearing. The machine has only to be raised at the handles and the carriage pushed under it so that

Fig. 287.—Ransomes' " Anglo-Paris No. 2 " Lawn-mower

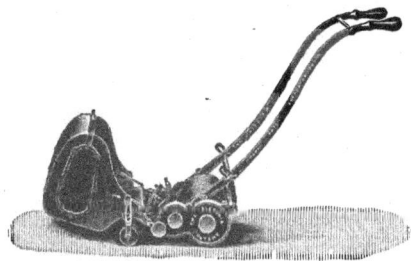

Fig. 286.—Caledonia Lawn-mower

of a similar character is the "Pennsylvania". Green's "Silens Messor" and Ransomes' "Patent Chain Automaton" are good examples of chain-action mowers. Shanks's "Britisher" and Ransomes' "Lion" and "Anglo-Paris No. 2" (fig. 287) are less expensive machines, suitable for small gardens. One of the features of their construction is the extreme simplicity. Under suitable conditions, they will give satisfactory service for long periods.

Motor lawn-mowers are now largely used where there are extensive lawns to be kept in order. They are economical and expeditious, and their management is not difficult. The largest sizes have a seat at the back for the driver (fig. 288), the smaller having handles which are held by a man walking behind (fig. 289). They are easy to turn and stop, the labour required being small.

the part of the machine in front of the rollers may rest on the wood cushion of the carriage. The machine is then lowered on to the carriage, and may be wheeled about with the greatest ease.

Hose-pipes (fig. 291).—A good supply of hose-pipes should form part of the equipment of every garden. Water should be

Fig. 290.—Lawn-mower Carriage

laid on wherever it is likely to be required, and either hydrants or stand-cocks placed at convenient intervals in all parts of the garden where there are plants that would require to be frequently watered in the absence of rain. It is best to get good stout hose of as large a bore as can con-

Fig. 288.—Shanks's 35-in. Motor Lawn-mower, with seat for driver

Fig. 289.—Shanks's 24-in. Motor Lawn-mower, with 4½-h.p. Engine

veniently be used. The wire-armoured hose is economical where it has to be dragged about much. When not in use it should be kept on a reel in a dry shed. The Lawn-Sprinkler (fig. 292) is useful for watering flower-beds, &c., or even as a substitute for a fountain. The Ball-nozzle Sprinkler (fig. 293) is an equally useful appliance, throwing out a spray similar to that shown in fig. 292. Royle's Tap-union (fig. 294) is a simple and

with wrought-iron frame and galvanized steel cistern and is largely used by Orchid-growers.

Sprayers.—The importance of a knowledge of how to overcome or prevent the wholesale destruction of garden crops by the attacks of insect and fungoid diseases has only recently been recognized in English horticulture. Special appliances are necessary to enable one to distribute an insecti-

Plain   Wire-armoured
Fig. 291.—Hose-pipes

Fig. 293.—Ball-nozzle Sprinkler

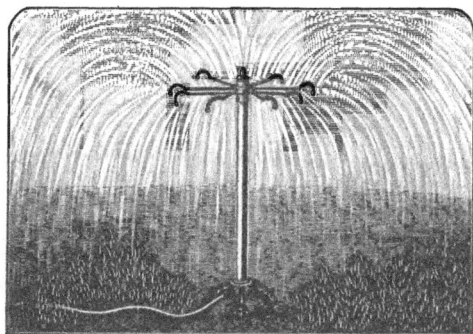

Fig. 292.—Lawn-sprinkler

Fig. 294.—Royle's Tap-union

excellent rubber contrivance for slipping on to taps instead of the cumbrous and often leaky crew-nozzle.

Watering Engines. — Of these there are many kinds used in gardens. They are made to act on the principle of the force-pump. One of the handiest of them is Green's Garden Engine (fig. 295).

Water-barrow. — An excellent form of water-barrow, by means of which several barrels can be in use at once, is shown at fig. 296. The stout iron pivot securely fixed to the sides of the barrel, drops into a slot formed on the ends of the iron frame. Another useful form (fig. 297) is made

cide over the whole of the trees in an orchard or a field of Potatoes, for instance, and these are now to be had, chiefly from French and American makers, who have invented various kinds of pumps, sprayers, &c., for this purpose. The "Knapsack Pump" (fig. 298), made of brass and copper, may be carried on the back and worked easily with one hand, whilst the other directs the spray delivered through a piece of hose a yard long. The other is the "Brass Spray Pump" (fig. 299), fitted into a galvanized-iron bucket, which may be easily carried about. In the more recent knapsack sprayers, air is pumped by pneumatic pressure into the receiver and, when the tap is turned on, the liquid is released automatically in a fine spray until the vessel is emptied. (See Vol. II, SPRAYING FRUIT-TREES.)

An excellent " Hand Vaporizer " (fig. 300) which holds 2 quarts of liquid, and is easily manipulated, distributing a vapour or spray

Fig. 295.—Green's Garden Engine

Fig. 296.—36-Gallon Water-barrow

in some gardens. It is light, moves easily, but makes a great noise, and does not wear nearly so well as a wooden one.

The *Navvy's barrow* is perhaps the best adapted for excavating or other work where planks are required. From its wide shallow form, it can be more easily loaded and emptied than barrows with deeper and more upright sides. The wheel is narrow, and made entirely of cast-iron, so that little soil adheres to it. In wet weather, and with clayey soil, wheeling on planks with a

Fig. 297.—Swing Water-barrow

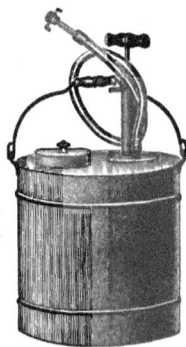

Fig. 299.—Spray Pump

in any direction, can be obtained from dealers in spraying machines. It can be used both for applying insecticides and for dewing Orchids, &c.

Barrows.—The common garden barrow is too well known to need description. A barrow of a different shape (fig. 301) is used in the market-gardens about London. With the exception of the wheels, it is such as a handy man can make in wet weather. The wrought-iron barrow (fig. 302) finds favour

broad wheel would be almost impracticable.

Hand-barrows.—These are easily made, the simplest being a shallow tray-like box 4 feet by 2 feet 3 inches, with the sides extending about a foot each way, and shaped to serve as handles. By adding short legs to this, it becomes what is called a fruit hand-barrow (fig. 303).

The *Truck Basket* (fig. 304) is handy for carrying small quantities of soil, &c., for which a barrow would be too large. It is made of thin strips of tough wood nailed on a stout frame, several sizes being supplied.

Fumigators. — Contrivances for applying tobacco-smoke and other fumes for the destruction of insects which infest plants. The principle is to apply it in such a way

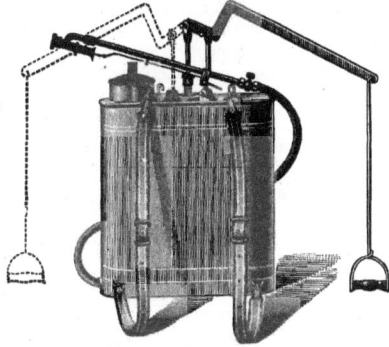

Fig. 298.—Knapsack Pump

that, whilst it is strong enough and remains about the plant long enough to destroy the insects, it does not injure the plant. The simplest method, when tobacco is to be used, is to make a hole in the side of a flower-pot, or, better still, an old zinc pail, near the bottom, so that the nozzle of a pair of bellows

Fig. 300.—Hand Vaporizer

can be introduced. A little live coal is put into the bottom of the pot, then tobacco-paper, and by gently blowing slow combustion is produced. An iron pot with a gridiron bottom, and a handle at the side like a saucepan, is a convenient utensil for this work. For very large houses, such as the Palm

House at Kew, a small portable forge, such as smiths use, is an excellent fumigator, as

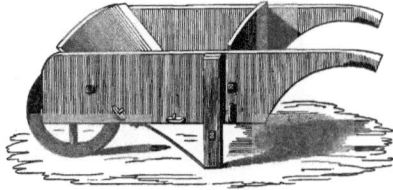

Fig. 301.—Box Barrow

it can be made to pour out large volumes of smoke with great rapidity.

One of the most efficacious of all fumi-

Fig. 302.—Wrought-iron Barrow

gators for small houses is Richards' XL-All Vaporizing Fumigator (fig. 305). It is a short cylinder, with a shallow saucer on top

Fig. 303.—Fruit Hand-barrow

containing a small quantity of compound (in cake or liquid form) simply evaporated by the agency of a spirit-lamp. It is extremely

Fig. 304.—Truck Basket

easy of application, certain in its effects upon insects, and quite harmless (with few exceptions) to the most tender foliage.

Sulphurator.—Since the attacks of mildew on the vine and other plants have become so prevalent, and as flowers of sulphur is the best-known remedy, sulphurators or "dredgers" have become very necessary.

Fig. 306.—Sulphurator

Fig. 305.—Richards' XL-All Vaporizing Fumigator

Powder Distributor, a rubber bag with a perforated nozzle (fig. 307), is useful for applying sulphur or tobacco powder, to use with one hand, manipulating the foliage or plant with the other.

Syringes are indispensable where there are glass structures for plants and forcing; and in small gardens they may be substituted to some extent for the garden engine, as regards fruit trees. There are many kinds, that shown in fig. 308 being a great improvement on the old form. The syringe is fur-

Accordingly, various kinds have been invented, some working with a wheel, on the principle of a fan, others like the bellows. Fig. 306 represents one which answers ex-

Fig. 307.—
Powder Distributor

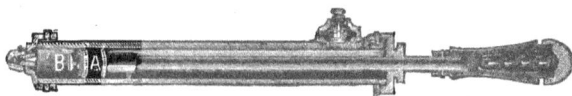

Fig. 308.—Garden Syringe (section)

Fig. 309.—Garden Syringe

ceedingly well. Other remedies are the specially prepared cones and sheets. The

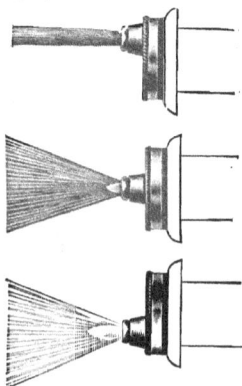

Fig. 310.—Triplex Rose

nished with two roses of different degrees of fineness, and a single tube when it is requisite to force out the water in one unbroken stream. These syringes are now fitted with a Patent Water-tight Plunger or Piston (fig. 308). The plunger can be compressed or loosened as required, being controlled by a thumb-screw (B). An improved "rose", attached to what is called White's Patent Triplex Syringe, is an ingenious arrangement of ball and nozzle which emits either a fine or coarse spray, or an unbroken stream, by slightly altering the position in which the syringe is held (see fig. 310). This rose has also been adapted for use upon a hose director. In using syringes, great care should be taken not to indent their sides through rough handling, as a single indentation renders the cylinder no longer a true one, and then the piston cannot fit accurately. In connection with syringes and spraying machines there are now a large variety of detachable bends and nozzles in use for distributing sprays of varying degrees of coarseness and fineness.

V. UTENSILS

Pots. — Flower pots are made of clay. They are sold in what are known as casts, the number in each cast being according to their size. The dimensions of the pots made in London and its vicinity are as follows:

NAME.	Number to the cast.	Diameter at top.	Depth.
		Inches.	Inches.
Twos, or 18-inch ..	2	18	14
Fours, or 15-inch ..	4	15	13
Sixes, or 13-inch ..	6	13	12
Eights, or 12-inch ..	8	12	11
Twelves, or 11-inch ..	12	11½	10
Sixteens, or 9-inch ..	16	9½	9
Twenty-fours, or 8-inch ..	24	8¼	8
Thirty-twos, or 6-inch.	32	6	6
Forty-eights, or 5-inch	48	4¼	5
Sixties, or 3-inch ..	60	3	3½
Eighties, or thumbs ..	80	2½	2½

the other hand, long tapering pots are not to be recommended. Generally, pots of large size are wider than they are deep; and on the contrary, the depth of small-sized pots equals or exceeds their width. Examples of the usual forms of plant pots, pans, and baskets are represented in fig. 311.

Drainage is provided for by a hole in the bottom, or in the side near the base.

It is frequently necessary, as a protection against slugs, beetles, &c., to isolate a plant by surrounding it with water. An excellent contrivance for this purpose is Warne's Protector, represented at fig. 312. The platform is open right through, and it is set in a dish which can be filled with water.

Besides the common forms, pots are made with double sides, with raised bottoms, also with projecting bases. The double-sided pot has a small opening at top by which the

Fig. 311

a, Orchid pot; *b*, Orchid pot (loose bottom); *c*, Perforated Orchid pot; *d*, Shallow suspending pan for Orchids; *e*, Suspending Orchid basket; *f*, Nest of pots, 1¾ to 30 in; *g*, Sea-kale pot; *h*, Rhubarb pot.

The various sizes of garden pots have one prevailing characteristic in their form, which is that of being wider at top than at bottom. This is necessary as, if the sides were perpendicular, the ball of earth could not be turned out without breaking the pot. Sandy soil, even without roots growing in it, could not by any means be pressed out of an earthenware cylinder, unless a very short one. On

space between the two sides can be filled with water, and thus the withdrawal of moisture from the soil by evaporation from the sides of the pot is prevented. But the same object is usually effected by placing one pot within another of a size or two larger, and stuffing the space between them with moss.

Flower-pots vary much in quality, according to the clay of which they are made, and the amount of burning they may receive. If soft—that is, slack burned—they absorb moisture too freely, become dirty frequently, soon getting coated with moss, and are, moreover, easily broken. On the other hand, some are too hard and brittle, and also break easily.

Pots suitable for plants intended to be planted in beds or borders can be made with a mixture of clay and cow manure, which after being shaped are only sun-dried, not baked. They last long enough, they afford additional food to the roots, and they may be set in the ground with ease.

Shallow pots and pans, the latter either square or round, of various sizes, are used in propagating. Rectangular pans, about 10 inches by 7 inches, are best for economiz-

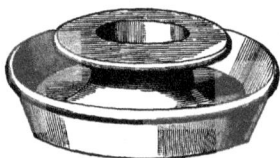

Fig. 312.—Warne's Plant Protector

ing space. Papier mâché pots in various sizes are used for raising seedlings that are to be transferred to the ground without disturbing the roots.

Earthenware Saucers or *Flats* are made of different sizes, to suit those of the pots which are placed in them. Glazed saucers for plants in rooms are sometimes made, and are preferable because they do not allow the water to pass through and cause damp on whatever they may be set.

The *Blanching Pot* (fig. 311, *g*, *h*) is used for blanching Sea-kale, Rhubarb, &c. It is an earthenware pot which is made in various shapes, and has a top which may be removed, so that the fitness of the vegetable for use may be ascertained without lifting the whole pot. Frequently common garden pots, with the hole in the bottom covered with a piece of slate or flat tile, are substituted for blanching pots, and answer the purpose very well.

Boxes or *Tubs* are used for large Bay trees, Palms, Camellias, Orange trees, &c. They are made of well-seasoned pine, oak, or teak, the price varying according to the material, teak being dearest. A useful plant tub, durable and cheap, may be made from a disused beer-cask, which a brewer will sell for a few shillings. This, when cut down

about one-fourth, the other end pierced, and painted green or brown, serves very well for a large plant in a conservatory. Slate is also sometimes used. Slate boxes possess the advantages of great durability, and of being easily kept clean and free from insects, to which they do not afford so many lurking-places as the wooden ones. They are, how-ever, not as good for many plants as those made of wood.

M'Intosh's Plant-box (fig. 313) has a neat appearance; and all its sides being

Fig. 313.—M'Intosh's Plant-box

movable, it offers greater facilities for re-moving the trees, examining their roots, replacing old soil with fresh, &c. Two of the sides, being hinged to the bottom, may be opened down by lifting up the iron bars; the others, which are not hinged, but lift up, may then be easily removed.

Round tubs made of pine, oak, or teak, after the style of that shown in fig. 314, are

Fig. 314.—Round Tub with ring or hook handles

best for general purposes, as they are easily made and are portable. The handles may be either as shown in the figure, or a pair of stout iron hooks may be screwed on to serve as handles. These are very convenient when the tub has to be lifted, a pair of poles being used as lifters.

Sieves and *Screens* are useful in gardens for sifting earth and for screening gravel, mould, &c. Sieves with very small meshes are also used for cleaning seeds.

All sieves should be what is termed square-meshed, varying from $1\frac{1}{2}$ inch to $\frac{1}{4}$ inch. This also applies to sieves used for seeds; the size of mesh in this case goes by number.

Grindstone.—The utility of a grindstone is such that it is said to be an accompaniment of civilization into the most remote parts of the world. It is indispensable in a garden, for when cutting tools are not properly sharpened the amount and quality of the work will be unsatisfactory. It would be well to have a large stone for spades, hoes, &c., and a smaller one of closer grit for fine-edged tools.

Watering-cans.—The common form of the watering-can with a straight rose, for open ground work, and smaller cans, with straight tubes of different lengths, but adapted for having either straight or bent-necked roses fixed upon them, will answer every purpose required of these utensils.

"Haw's Improved Watering-can" is an improvement on the ordinary type, and is much preferred on account of its strength and handiness. The large pots have a galvanized hoop round the bottom, which imparts strength and durability. Fig. 315 illustrates the various sizes and shapes, all designed on the same principle. Excellent roses are supplied with these cans.

The 3-gallon and 4-gallon water-carriers are most useful and convenient for the purpose intended.

Fig. 316.—Heathman's Extension Ladder

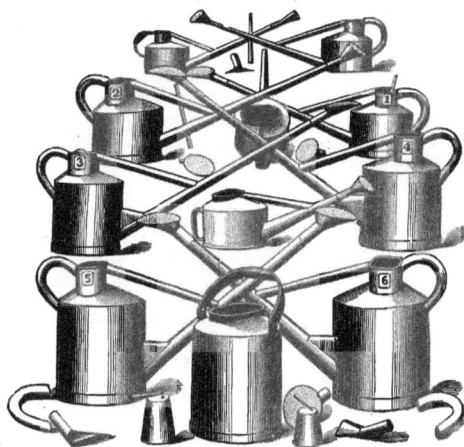

Fig. 315.—Haw's Watering-cans

Ladders.—Various kinds of these are required in gardens and orchards. For wall-trees, a step-ladder, with boards for steps, is far preferable to one with rounds. The sides and steps should be made of clean well-seasoned deal, and at the top two iron spurs should be attached to the sides, for the steps to rest on when they are placed against the wall, that the trees may not be injured. Folding-steps are useful in green-houses. Ladders have been made for orchard work with two strong supports, connected by iron stays from one support to the other, and from the supports to each side of the ladder; it is thus rendered self-supporting. Extension ladders (fig. 316) are useful for work requiring a self-supporting ladder, but are too heavy and cumbersome for market-garden or orchard work.

Packages.—A great variety of baskets, boxes, &c., may now be obtained, in many sizes, for the conveyance of garden produce. A chapter on the subject of packing flowers, plants, &c., will be found elsewhere.

VI. MISCELLANEOUS ARTICLES

Tallies.—No mode of numbering plants can excel that in which the Arabic figures are employed; for these being the most universally known can be more easily read, and with less risk of mistake, than any other. But, in many cases, painting numbers in a manner not liable to be soon effaced by exposure to the weather would occupy too much time, and would prove too expensive. Accordingly, marks to represent numbers are cut on wood, and these cuts remain visible till the wood gets into a state of complete decay. The use of Roman figures (I, V, X, &c.) is not uncommon in nurseries, the difficulty of making C (100) being got over by substituting a notch on the edge of the tally. Thus

would represent 126. Many nurserymen use old wheel spokes as tallies as they last for years. A number, corresponding with that opposite the name of the plant in the stock book, is usually stencilled in black on a white painted surface, and will serve to indicate any special kind or variety until it is no longer stocked.

For ordinary use nothing has been invented to supersede the prepared pine-wood label, slightly rubbed with white paint, and written upon with a black-lead pencil whilst wet. Some composition pencils, of which the marks on paper cannot be effectually rubbed out by india-rubber, are preferable to those of genuine plumbago. Red chalk is found to withstand the weather for many years.

The best permanent label for trees and shrubs is a slab of sheet-lead, 4 inches by 3 inches, or 3 inches by 2 inches, with about ½ inch of one long side turned over to form a rim, below which two holes are pierced. The surface of the lead should be beaten smooth, and then the letters punched in with punch-type, obtained from an iron-monger. When printed, the letters should be filled up with white-lead, and when this is dry the whole surface should be rubbed with an oiled rag. A little practice is required to get the letters nicely arranged. The label should be attached to the plant by means of a piece of iron wire. This label (see fig. 317) is used exclusively at Kew for all trees and shrubs in the open. A form of it is used also for labelling herbaceous and alpine plants in the rock-garden, where wooden labels large enough to be durable are unsightly. The lead label is practically indestructible, and although not cheap compared with wood, it is at least as in-expensive as the other so-called in-destructible labels.

Fig. 317.—Lead Label

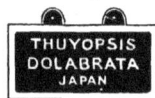

White celluloid labels are largely used. They are written on with an ordinary lead pen-cil or with a pre-pared ink, and both writing and label will last for years. Small porcelain labels with a green face, written on with black ink, and afterwards glazed, are fixed in metal clips, and are used for plants in rock-gardens, &c.

The " Acme " cast labels (fig. 318) are made of stout zinc, with raised letters on a black ground. They are supported on stiff wire stems, or have a pair of eyes for sus-pending by wire or nail-ing to a wall. Where the lead label cannot conveniently be made, the Acme or some such permanent label should be used. These, with names printed, are only made to order. The " Imperishable Strat-ford " label differs from the Acme in being made of a white metal with the raised letters in black (fig. 319).

A very excellent zinc label called "The Ideal" is made with stout zinc, having four holes at

Fig. 318.— " Acme" Cast Label

Fig. 319.—" Imperishable Stratford " Label

Fig. 320.—General View of French Garden and Vegetable Farm at Henwick, near Newbury: showing Cloches, Glass Frames, &c.

the corners. When fixed on thin wire stems they have a neat appearance. The writing on the zinc face is done with a neatly pointed stick or quill pen dipped in acid. The face of the zinc should be rubbed bright with emery-paper before being written upon.

Parchment labels used to be very generally employed for the temporary labelling of plants, but they were soon affected by the weather—in damp weather getting into a state of pulp, and in dry weather shrivelling up. They are now superseded by a very excellent card-like label, made from what is termed " Manila substances ". Another composition label, known as the " Ivorine Label ", and which is of thick celluloid substance, is now largely used for labelling

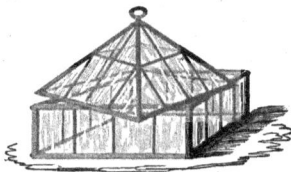

Fig. 321.—Hand-glass

pot plants, especially Orchids. It is said to be imperishable and unbreakable, and it can be written upon by either pencil or pen, the writing being indelible, except when well rubbed with soap. This label can be obtained from any dealer in horticultural sundries.

Nail Bag.—A bag or large pocket for holding nails and shreds, whilst nailing wall-trees, &c., may either be made of stout close canvas or of leather. In the latter case it sometimes contains one or two small pockets for knives. It is suspended by shoulder straps, and further secured by a belt. All this may be necessary in nailing against very high walls; but in ordinary cases, the canvas answers the purpose sufficiently well, and is at all times more pliable.

Hand-glasses are made in various shapes, their bases being generally square, hexagonal, or octagonal; but now that glass is cheap, and that sheet-glass can be obtained of sizes corresponding with those of the sides, the preference is given to hand-glasses with only four sides. The framework is usually constructed of lead, copper, or cast-iron; the

latter (fig. 321), if kept painted, answers well, and is very durable and convenient.

Bell-glasses and cloches (fig. 322) are used for protecting and hastening the growth of vegetables, &c. Others of less size, and made of whiter glass, are employed in propagating. An excellent substitute for a bell-glass is a seed-pan half-filled with soil in which cuttings or seeds are placed, the top being covered with a pane of glass large enough to fit the pan. This is easily ventilated and can be tilted slightly to prevent drip.

Fig. 322.—Cloche

The *Aphis Brush* (fig. 323) is useful for removing aphides from Roses and other plants. The handle is of steel, and elastic. By the pressure of the fingers on one side, and that of the thumb on the other, the brushes are brought together upon the shoot to be cleaned, and the aphides are removed without injury to the plant.

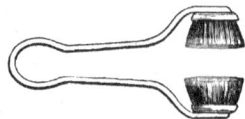

Fig. 323.—Aphis Brush

Tying Materials.—The one in most general use is Raffia fibre. This is obtained from the leaves of an African palm, *Raphia Ruffia*. It is a very strong soft pliable material, not unlike the old Russian bast, but far superior, although it does not last long if allowed to rest on damp soil, or in any damp situation. It should be hung up in the driest parts of store-room to keep it in good condition ready for use. Tar string for tying trees and shrubs, securing Roses, &c., to stakes, should also be kept in stock.

Various other articles are required in a garden, such as planks for wheeling; canvas, gauze, and nets of twine for protecting seeds and fruits from birds and other pests; wall nails and shreds, copper wire, willows for tying, mats, stakes for plants, thermometers, &c. A selection of carpenter's and glazier's tools can be made good use of by a handy man, thereby often saving time as well as expense.

www.ingramcontent.com/pod-product-compliance
Lightning Source LLC
Chambersburg PA
CBHW031227090426
42740CB00007B/738